Chronicle Stardust

Shruti Yadav

First Published in October 2020

ISBN: 978-93-90396-35-1

BLUEROSE PUBLISHERS
www.bluerosepublishers.com
info@bluerosepublishers.com
+91 8882 898 898

Cover Design:
Anu Krishna

Typographic Design:
Namrata Saini

Distributed by: BlueRose, Amazon, Flipkart, Shopclues

Winds know their trait to reach the destination,
And so our heart.
Water masters to silent the shores,
And so our mind.
Fire adapts the good and evil,
And so our soul.
Sky discern, boundaries are diabolical,
And so our life.
The soil seeks the change of the world, yet it hail!
And so do we.
Five elements of nature are the five candour of life.

-Shruti Yadav

Preface

I started writing when I was fifteen year old. I use to scribble my line of thinking, notions and theories and jotting down them on papers. Doing that often, it became my habit. It was my father who encouraged me, to write poetries and get them published. There was my English teacher at that time, whom I used to show my writings, and she always had that amaze look on her face after reading them. She was enraptured with the tone of words I portrayed. I discerned different version of life in conflicting colours of environment and people. Experiences and challenges made my poetries better, and from then I kept them closer to my heart as they sometimes expressed me in limited boundaries.

Poetries are not something you think and put down, I feel it's a part of flow in your life. Until you feel the words it can never convey the messages. For me, when I see something whether it is positive, negative or neutral, I think about it inwards and comprehensively and that's what make me combine the feelings and pour it down into words. As many people, it was easier for me to write than expressing, though, I am a Law graduate, and speaking and listening are my great accomplishments.

Inspiration in life is very important, and I have bag full of them around me which is not only limited to people. If you are a writer, you may get incentivised from tiniest to infinity.

Acknowledgement

It is a poetry book which whirls around life, romance, love and many utterly feeling that are silent may be inside or outside of you. We have a beautiful life, which is also a part of many lives and those people may sometimes offer great choices to you. Writing was my and my parents choice too. I believe parents are the first step in everything you do in life, they not only encourage you but also give you a ride through the entire journey.

My father, always aspired me to become a Civil Officer someday, but he never curbed me from writing poetries or any of my hobbies. He was the one who inspired me to write and get them publish.

My mother, one of my closest advisor. My whole family, had been a big support for me always and I can never exclude my closest friends. I thank Bluerose Publication for providing me with this platform and helping me throughout the journey.

More profoundly, I thank my vicinity. The surroundings are so important to convert the feeling into words.

About the Author

SHRUTI YADAV is a 1996 born, presently living and educated in Lucknow. She is a Law graduate in the year 2020 from NLU, Visakhapatnam. Writing and painting art is her passion and part of life. She has great achievements in paintings and designing and is following her dreams in writings also. This is her first book for poetry publication. She is passionate about history, mythology and selected literatures. Her writing are not majorly confined to one pole or direction. She is a metaphorical writer. Genre is lyrical poetry.

Poetries

It Was Not a Mere Survival

The words within me are sharp,
Lurking and seeking the noise.
Whispering the silence creeps me, retrieves me for knowing the minimal,
I have never commiserated the truth.
Summoned by knife, slaughtered in the veins of false,
Sky does not gives you hopes,
It's the soils that calls you inside.
Butchered by my own thoughts in the valley of destiny,
Cuffed by the uproar that has loosen the grip of satisfaction.
Do you know the sobriety of living a sloshed life?
With the sight of fake synonyms,
The texture of drained soul and laugh of shadow faces.
I am a road to no exit, to no bullets in heart yet dead,
When life suffocates, it folds you in its mirage,
It's you, your norms, your circles and its words.
I would have climbed the passive stairs in this era,
Thou, it takes more than coins to live.
It was not a mere survival,
It was more to the procastrination of verisimilitude.

You Stood in a Shadow with Drunken Eyes

Water flows to the zenith without asking the shore to hold it,
Love bleeds to death without asking earth to soak it,
Wind blows to horizon without knowing where it's heading to.
The flows in your words may be soft but they pierce like a sword,
You talk about faith, I talk about us,
You talk about misery, I talk about love,
You talk above me, I talk within you.
The fear inside me never faded,
You bought lamps to burn them up,
Though they disappeared but left a scar.
Scar that manifest the outer me and inner you,
I never found you on a way where I always wanted you,
You stepped on me with a fire and asked why did I turn into ashes,
You grabbed my throat deliberately and asked me why I couldn't breathe with you,
I walked away the ages just to find you,
You stood in a shadow with drunken eyes.

I Was a Visitor to My Own Mind

Did you ever try to source out good from bad?
Truth from a lie,
Basic from neutrality,
It becomes hard when you don't,
Or may be harder when you cannot.
Its more to itself when you know the world around,
With less concern or maybe more feathers,
Degrading and inglorious it is when you lose the grip of survival,
Figuring out life wasn't an easy task,
You work day and night to find living,
But the shoes you are wearing becomes sole-free.
You have to rug your feet to move forward,
Life has never threatened anyone, to believe in its existence,
And so, does the death.
You are mocked around for just being yourself,
You are lifted by none but sanded by many.
And that's all what contributes in describing what's around and living,
Because it all became dark at a point,
My heart did shatter,
And I was a visitor to my own mind.

We Fought Enough, without Framing the Dreams

We fight battles, from the blue to the stars,
We fight destiny, losing ourselves,
We fight heart, brave enough to stand,
We walk streets to figure out what is written for us.
Though we never cared enough to stand and give a read,
Its not always easy to rush in the middle of the thorns dressed in pearls,
Life seeks all, we learn the hardships, irrespective we deal with it or not,
We make ourselves adhere,
Closing our eyes to what is coming with a blaze,
What we cared, was only what brings high shoes, Rugged was never our choice.
Between if and but we lost chronic,
We lost us, in the journey of nowhere.
And what really matters was it never mattered,
We fought enough, without framing the dreams,
We are fighting to know the uncertain path,
We will fight for survival.

Feather, to an Audacious Flight

What we dream of, remains in the curtail of entity,
Farthest to the grain, nearest to the vein.
Moulding the rhythm of songs,
We find our own music sung to none,
We speak aloud expecting others to listen the fantasy.
Fantasy created in the howl of flexibility,
Woven in our own heart, Destroyed in our own arms.
We perish our identity to create one,
We seek the bird lost in the tranquillity of her weakness.
She flew to the vicinity of her own home just to find another,
Carrying a mirror that reflected different norms, Faking the materialistic reality.
She got none to show her, the other side,
Flattering truths and blissful lies.
Bound in her own feet, less did she know she got something more than the sight.
Feather, to an audacious flight.

The Map on My Skin

I stood on an unknown road,
Knowing life and death.
Its my scars that make me believe that I lived,
I remember how expensive was life,
What I don't, whom I mocked and traded it to,
I remember the oceans floors that flooded my dreams,
What I don't, who gulped the innocence.
I remember the serene and purest mind,
What I don't, who killed the song and who choked the throat.
The strokes on my palm were the sign of integrity,
Who made them, was a malicious thought.
The salt to my scars were the people I loved,
They moralised, knifed and turned it to ashes.
The door next to me was blocked,
The roof fell and someone died.
Died for the hopes, for music to none, for sharp tone to a broken ear,
Died in the black and white, by drowned mazed souls,
Who came were true, who came-acted they could hear.
They offered linen to design the scars,
Extended roses to cover the red,
None could see below it, what could the red soil even call for.
Standing on that road, breeze through my hair,
What Stuck, was me and what left, was within me.
They loved the world, may be I was not a part of it,
To seize space there I drew thousand lines,
The map on my skin.

The Day I Started Dreaming, I Had the Entire World

What do you see when you wake up,
Don't you realise that the stars went faded?
That the moon went back,
Or the sun was born again.
You realised the claustrophobic you,
You realised that the pillow on which you whined was still warm,
You realised that you were left with none,
None to hold you across the fidelity of survival.
Maybe, you realised that the entire universe was just not for you,
Though it was hard to forget, the soul called to surrender,
But You didn't have to give up,
Rushing through the streets you figure that even the flickering light even usher,
Smiling was just not as painful as allowing someone to murder, even if it is of yours,
Winds were hard to resist when they padded the leaves,
From one end to another.
The day I started dreaming I had the entire world
World beyond sight, world beyond perception.
Tarnishing the soul more was just not an option.

Stand on the Spine of the World Crest

Slowly the morning started whilst the darkest hour,
Slowly the light penetrated within the shedded roof,
Slowly the curtains were lifted within the sturdy walls.
Old skin sometimes does not tell the temperature in the vicinity,
Its has became beyond time and reckless truth.
What age makes you is the simplicity of life,
What it mould you into is the intricacy of past.
The weather have painted itself in dolour,
Some white, some black and some slight tinge.
Awaking the bright colours of young is no option in hand,
What we retain in our soul is earned from our birth land.
We may have broken the chains of our society in twenties,
Then why, we surrender to it in seventies.
We may have caused terror in our lives in twenties,
Then why, we become tranquil in seventies.
We may have boosted compassion till depth,
Then why, we give up on life so easily.
Passing through the time desires more than we can give it,
What it holds, mattered more to you than to unknown vicinity.
Smothering the light till it extinguish is no hard dance.
Burning yourself with lamp brings eternal spark,
Stand on the spine of the world crest,
Let them realise what makes them stronger.

There Were None

The day I opened my eye,
I thought nothing.
The life around me was waving back,
As if something has crossed the amazon,
Walking half the road of life you realise that there were none of them standing to shadow you,
They bestowed doldrums.
Was the calling of life, just the miracle of god's hand or I had a purpose.
Mount your head upwards,
Realise you broke the chains of infinity and crawling towards the end.
Still the sky remains clouded and you see everything.
The tunes of your radio should have words
They communicate,
Maybe you just had no listener,
The lines of your palms are leading spotless but there were none.
None to see you,
None to pray,
None to curb pain,
None to break that constant gaze of your eye.

Bleed the Truth of Immortality

One does want to be calm in the hover of philosophy,
Waving white flags and singing nightingales will only
adjourn the present case.
What happens in the night is dark and timid,
Everyday the moon does not turn red,
Everyday the tides are not high,
Everyday situations are not so indistinguishable,
Everyday the balance of rising and falling are not equal.
We opt for solutions when answer always lies in the
question,
We opt for hustle where pain is just an assumption,
Facing the authenticity of false, as people continue to wrap it in
lenin,
What we see, what we seek and what we soak,
Remains on the weight of words we carry.
I have turned my head away from many proclaimers of
serenity,
I have broken the chains of many stereotypes and
deciphered the righteousness that existed mythically.
I rose from that soil which was blood soaked from the
humanity's contentment,

But even after I lack my soul, I bind myself with self-
worth.
What is live, what is living and what has been lived,
Remains on what destiny is defined for us.

Life would be moulding itself in forms and norms,
In sunken states, in sloth arms.
What is truth, what is false and what is correct,
Remains in shadow of hollowness.
One does roam to seek the exact veracity,
But no one bleeds the truth of immortality.

Grave Ourselves with Candour

I have always asked myself the truth behind life,
Truth which was always masked.
Life that is not entirely yours,
Life that is folded in the arms of a diabolic world.
When we walk the shores do we realise,
That the water splashing our feet have crossed lengths and ages to reach there just to touch it's ending,
When we watch the clouds thundering and humming around,
Do we realise, the enormous water it is carrying,
Gulping it from the ocean.
The sparkles in our vicinity may not glitter for others,
My dimensions are small, my hatred is nugatory,
Thou, I speak for them, I fashion silence for me.
Nudging the situation will not make it look back to you,
You have to stand in front of it making it weak.
I will ogle you until you shut your eyes and see me no more,
I will not extinguish the fire until you turn into ember and scatter around in the darkness,
I maybe a broken window with glasses that are moulding themselves into a shield.
Strength my sword, shall cut the words down that have roused directly on me,

Respect and self-importance, for that I have lived for yet,
Mumbling from another corner will not subdue my thoughts,
Living in the age of morally correct trauma,
We need to decide what's in our favour and what is not.
Whether we stand in the line of speculation,
Or grave ourselves with candour.

Every Word they Said Stretched Distant and Bygone Errand

Those little hands that shrouded the cloth on pyre,
Those naked eyes that had lost the sight, unfolded and lucid.
Masking all his thoughts and unwinding the thirst of truth,
Airy, was the vicinity and the sun was roaring hard.
It hardly took one breathe to get him alive,
and so was not allowed,
The blue around was downhearted,
None could adhere his acceptance, none were speaking sharp.
What existed in the dark lamp a night before was gone,
What vanished was his own part,
What summoned her was his own God.
He couldn't question any mortal,
He couldn't answer the dead,
Who was laying was his mother,
who were crying were just someone.
Broken was not the word for him, he was just seven and his life was miserly done,
The most difficult time comes when we question ourselves,
With reckless answers and unguided truth.

Who would he even ask, what will he chase,
He was just a string in a tangled world.
He was woken by the cries of people,
in the room he will never visit,
Wrapped in a blanket of peace,
in a space where he will never fit.
Was he draped, inculpating him in the quietus of his mother,
Was he drawn in the shallow destiny of the society.
They took his innocence in the lore of living,
His penance had to be made impacted to others.
He grew in the maze drawn for few,
Reminding him of his malefaction and deaf thoughts.
Pondering on every sweat he made, realising his illusory land,
Every day he fought his demons and lost inside out,
Every word they said stretched distant and bygone errand.

I Rise, Taste My Own Ash, to Walk a Mile

The walls of our home were painted blur and bright,
Promising and failing in its own nature.
Thy, ravishing were the bricks in here,
No one knew its inner wailing.
Not much were the talks shared between us,
We only delighted the nights,
And quietened the days.
The warmness blackened and fluttered somewhere, someplace else,
Where stars were dull and the sky was bright,
There were no mirror to our broken souls, we could see in each others eye.
Every day passed smouldering us apart, Was it he, me or us.
What had to be shared was long gone,
What was left were the dolls and all the magic had vanished,
Behind the curtains were simple eyes with no emotions,
Emotions that once touched every inch of me.
May be the clock was ticking too fast,
May be all the gratifying moments have passed.
Maybe I was plainly a sojourn,
May be, I am the lamp that had escalated the darkness on him.
All seemed Unsettled and I left.
I left behind the doors that were never open for me.
Ignited, eyes closed, letting tongues of fire eat me alive,
I rise, taste my own ash, to walk a mile.
None did stop, none did speak,
What was left was also unheard.

Mock from their Faces

They already decided that I was a misfortune,
Rendering the vocals, and breathing the heaviest,
I could only accept it.
Ambience, showed the gravity of hatred,
No one knew the bloating of my pain,
I could never make choices for my life.
Because every choice followed the path where I never wanted to land,
They already decided that things were not right with me,
But no one knew the versions within me.
Things were simply not adverse,
Deep dives to hell and heaven was a part, too.
Life was not that fermenting,
It has taken bridges across the oceans, just to find pension of serenity.
They already decided that I had no reason to live,
Far they knew I had many, but the many never wanted me.
I can steal the sky, though not the mock from their faces,
I always laid hardships, life was always beyond repercussions.
Never ask the stars about its existence it may lose its luminary,
And may be so did I.

I Am All Sewn Up

Measuring the darkest days,
Covering the smallest smile.
How life goes on, it's little bit described.
Speaking the unseen thoughts,
Beautifying the ugliest self,
How life seeks, it's a little bit described.
Walking the simplest road,
Hiking the toughest height,
How life grows, it's a little bit described.
Smaller days bear larger importance,
Larger the wrongs carried smaller repentance,
How life thinks, it's little bit described.
Pushing the dreams in hollow escape,
Waking up with empty hands,
How life sleeps, it's bit described.
Digging in the forest of riches,
Falling in a pit of failures,
How life turns, it's a little bit described.
What life pledge, is it's duty,
Into what it's framed, is our responsibility,
How life learns, its little bit described.
I am sewn up Into cuts and maps,
I am an alluring mended patch of worth,
How life fits in, it's little bit described.

When Silence Speaks

It all started with a call,
I was walking with bare feet like on the fresh grass.
Less did I know that it was a sage of dead's,
With every steps, the leaves broke it's bone,
Yellow, green, orange, it all turned pale.
It was hard to adjust there, you blink and the ambience change,
Grey was colour it carried, shivering was the atmosphere that bounded it.
Hello! I spoke, he is gone-said the voice from other side,
In no time, the life fell beyond him.
Though Ambiguous yet silence spoke a lot.

Sidewalk Love

I said I love you,
Putting everything at stake in just three words.
He looked at me like it was an assault,
I knew the pain within my soul was unseen by him,
I grabbed my pen,
But instead of writing on papers,
I stabbed him with my words.
No one saw it coming even if it was in plain
sight-not even him, certainly not him.
I always thought it would have to be a storm,
To make a ship capsize,
I didn't know three words were enough to make a person
jump the hedges,
To leave the wheels un-commanded until ship sinks,
To Leave the life crashed into a sea boulder.
But altogether things merge, remaining silent on what was
unsaid,
Then where did it all go
Was it a sidewalk love?

To the Fairytale

Wondering if the sky was dark or it just became blind
with the coming shadow,
Wondering if the stars were pure or they also peeped to
the naked space,
Wondering if the moon had marks or it became
someone's slave.
It was all blank and gone,
The fire within was more tempting than the vicinity.
Footprints were marking the path,
Path that led somewhere, where destination was even
ambiguous.
They are mocking for my existence, I was fighting for my
presence,
Among several I stood alone, I stood devastated,
Among thousands I stood calm, I stood hope,
Raising a toast for my life to eternity.
For the life which slipped down the mud,
None came to ask, all came to blame,
The wind told it clear, everything gets wrapped one day,
In the arms of tranquillity.
The air swayed and bloomed the eye to the new morning,
The rays were high and warm, smirking the essence,
and the Dreams flourished to the fairy-tale.

Loneliest Crowd

You told me the truth,
Unseen unspoken,
I knew the hearts within us shattered long back,
But hoping doesn't take deep dives.
Walking on the same paths never led us to the same corner,
Togetherness was mere a grief.
The question of fading love was still unanswered,
The scar of knowing you was still unsaid.
Somewhere the darkness became dense,
Still the light penetrated.
Wind carried us along,
Below the waves, above the sky,
But the heart was still un-sided.
Some answers were still disclosed,
Her last breath was sourcing,
Among the loneliest crowd.

Until Next Time

Existence is that what we really talk about,
Beyond the lights what we see, is it the darkness,
Or the same hazy life we always dreamt of.
We may walk in the sunlight, burning our self to the ashes,
But we never crawl in the shade because we fear dark.
Darkness has always been protruding,
Embossing our fear which does not
have stand on the floor.
Black never bought death and white never bought life,
It's the mind that bargains the heart,
Black were the souls that brightened the modesty.
Whites were the honour to honesty,
Though the difference lies none.
World is connected beyond the contradictions of the shades,
We stump to realise it now or may be until next time.

I Was a Mere Puppet: Insight

They were talking silently but I could hear the whispers hard,
They folded the palms to hide the lie, I could barely see the dust falling,
They fastened the belt to leave the world, I was hiding under the bed in dark,
They could see the rainbow frozen, I could feel the thundering light.
The ice within was melting, though the fire already extinguished,
World was playing truth and dare, with question only of atrocities.
I had answer to none, none to quench their mind,
None to settle at the basic of all,
None, where words were not enough.
World, where my hair flick was enough to prove my character,
World that took security to keep you at peace,
It can roll you from the horizon to the poll,
Crossing oceans, rocks and woods.
Thou, wondering the passing of nights,
While, walking in the middle, illuminating the sky.
Agathokakological, their words moulded my life,
Distinguished and futile to the vicissitude,
I was a mere puppet, insight.

Flavours of Life

I was craving hard, harder than ever,
Shattered in a box of guilt or innocence, unknown to me.
You came like a magic of heaven,
I was dusk of the hell, known to world, unknown to oneself.
I came to the world with none, here, I am stepping back with none,
You stayed close, I remained unbothered.
It was not you that threatened me,
It was love, love that already blew my soul from the shore to the deep.
I wasn't amazed, it already happened,
We both wanted me, either had to lose.
We both fought for my existence,
Differed there, as you craved for love above my heart, I craved for life below my feet
How will all sustain?
Neither you nor I was aware of the fortunes, baking every bit of our longlines,
With the flavours of life,
You came in light I was dressed in black,
You grabbed my hand, so did the death to the ashes.

They Cared, but None Cared Enough

The shallow water always taught me, how much depth it saw,
Someone who does not know how to swim will get drowned easily.
You can't lend a hand to a person who has already forgotten his extremes,
We cannot make love to someone who is already intimidating.
Stars cannot fall on earth seeking bright light within darkness of humans,
Earth cannot sink itself knowing sky is the only existence.
Shattered body cannot be brought back by simply blowing its life,
We have moved in a world that cannot subside itself just because someone trimmed its shore.
We still have deep dives left,
People may seem close enough.
Try reaching your hand to them,
The shadow will just flourish, flourish to zenith, among the stars,
They love you outside the core, you are lost inside the crust.
They live with you and you are dead within,
Every word seemed like a dagger,
Piercing through, with no existence,
They cared, but none cared enough.

Through the Light Behind the Darkness

That day it rained, it rained a lot,
Water was deep, sky was dark,
That road witnessed it all.
The beauty, the shadow and the silent tears,
Rain was whispering, wind flowing through her hair,
What was broken, remained broken.
Thundering just shared the sorrows, sorrows that bought darkness.
She gazed till the end, discerning through drops,
Breathing heavily and sighing high,
That road witnessed it all.
Lamps were flickering as if the atmosphere was drunk,
Sky cried loud and so did she.
Water ripped the soil and so did her tears,
No call for peace, everything just vanished.
Hidden in robe of eternity, there stood a figure,
Never knew, for holding or saving her,
Maybe it was late, late enough to love.
The soil got deep red,
Her veins became furious, blood spilled and so her love.
So...Did she die or woken up in another world,
That road witnessed it all,
Through the light behind the darkness.

Do We Still Have to Live?

Look at the gazing sun, does it look similar?
Nothing seems alike, may be the rays walked away,
Where is that hope, where did it all go,
You taught me a lot.
You never lived to anyone's expectations,
Expectations that were regardless your needs,
The stones on my path aren't leisure.
I must shed blood, I have to stay awake and walk until I reach infinity,
Until I find what I always wanted to see when I wake up every morning.
Distances are just numbers,
Only the measure of your smile counts,
Every night you fall apart but its moon which slays your part.
We don't have to shine all day,
Our karma prevails us.
Life never talks about rough,
Sometimes getting broken limbs gives tougher challenges to a person to live,
For which he achieves the stairs to zenith.
Do we talk about living the way we wanted?
We never saturate our self, we only talk about the shadow below the naked truth.
For that, do we still have to live?

Hitched with the Soil

Waving my hand towards the sky,
Bought nothing, but my existence was may be watching me from there.
I could never catch a fallen star,
Maybe I should unfold my spirit,
And cover my wrath in the universe.
My heart was craving for his breath,
Though far engulfing the surroundings, I could hear only mine.
Never have I, Hitched with the soil,
We had our promises and differences,
Battle and songs were sung hard,
It swallowed every blood of his.
Earth could cry his valorous tears,
What could soil do more after flapping him into her arms with the bravest of souls.

When Life Made No Sense

The glory in our veins flow until we question it,
Time, held in a blank space, what circles it are empty,
Fathoming and immortalising our persistence.
Hours passed by,
Difficult were the question raised, more was our value,
Bound in the folds of criticism, I had to stand true,
It raises the smoke and extinguishes the esteem.
Society binds you in threads of expectations,
Feels like a morning splash but ends in the pool of regret,
Painting the crust and disintegrating the core.
We erode them having no roof above us,
We sweep them knowing the dust falls into our space.
In the cosmos, we are responsible for our truth,
Truth is not a strangers mind, it solemnise on what you think,
Truth is aura, false is contagious,
Truth stands holding your back and makes you fall when defiled.
Thou, life is pale, life is never black,
Watching the streets clenching anonymously to what,
Some will stare and some had grasped the sky,
Shall we walk in the dense lie.
I grabbed my shoes and got out of the line,
Far end the road I could not see but I was clear,
I walked laughing, I can crawl in despair.
The challenges and smiles were tough and immense,
I had to stand even when life made no sense.

His Lust Mislead My Love

When you can live to feel his warmth, is love,
When you can live to make him remember, the core essence within the soul, is love,
When you can live to make the beautiful feeling the part of your life, is love.
Question of love and life are tangled in the box of doom.
Where secret lies in the truth of life and much of love,
Where the reality coincides the mocking faces,
My love for him was simple in the world's creed.
It was bloomed in the heavenly womb and nurtured in a gracious song,
Song, sung in the darkest space of my life,
Song, that was more than expression to me,
Song, which purely expound you in me.
World was a conundrum in disguise and
You were the evasive path,
What I had known was the same that I should know,
Promises were made and hung on the hook,
Suspended until the wall fell and submerged it.
To whom was he loyal, me or my flesh,
To whom would I have answered to me or my flesh,
Some energies are dark and sharp.
Piercing the thought and hollow the core,
That was no love,
His lust mislead my love.

I Have Lost My Heart to You

Whether yes or no,
The sky will fall apart irrespective you hold it or leave it,
I may walk ages, above time, below universe,
Running towards life or crawling with death.
There was a time when I used to
think that we hold our destiny,
Though in no time I found the truth.
Some believe we make our own,
some have left them to Lord,
Here, we stand knowing nothing for a life,
All we are doing is surviving the stroke of something that
is unleashing us.
The world gave us life, life that had you,
You, although not mine, but enough
to what I can call to be drunk on.
There are phases when we see darkness,
You bought light directly through my soul, which broke
the silence into pieces,
Every breathe justifies you in me,
Every blink reminded me just to see you,
To the oath in lord's arm,
I have lost my heart to you.

Sunny Days and Blossomed Flowers

Mother, I am on the road ahead,
Failing back, tumbling slowly and walking the yellow leaves.
She tried to race the winds to reach her,
Walk fast was she told from her slow feet,
Hurry! The words echoed centring the avenue trees.
Beautiful day with smooth winds,
Leaves swaying, singing the heavens wing,
Smells of lavender and purple.
Rain made the woods green and life was so simple,
Breathings were slow, inhaling the essence of nature,
Twirling and spinning in the long gowns,
Women's wondered everywhere.
Sara and her mother went on the roads for picking the flowers,
The atmosphere was religious, with the crimson on the Gods,
Season of bliss, rain of dalliance and smell of love.
Rays covered like a blanket on earth and soaked all its gloom,
Aroma of jasmine and lily,
Flooding the vicinity untainted and fragrance bound beautifully.
The world was a picture to magical,
And became lust to beauty,
Thundering clouds came with striking flares.
They went home, seeking the nature in its own way,
Sometimes God converge its unknown viewers,
Bringing Sunny days and blossomed flowers.

9 789390 396351

Printed by Libri Plureos GmbH in Hamburg, Germany